Things I Need, Things I Want

Mike Biehn

ROSEN COMMON CORE READERS

Rosen Classroom™

New York

Published in 2013 by The Rosen Publishing Group, Inc.
29 East 21st Street, New York, NY 10010

Book Design: Michael Harmon

Photo Credits: Cover Tom Burlison/Shutterstock.com; pp. 4, 6 (house) V.J. Matthew/Shutterstock.com; p. 4 (clothes) Mike Flippo/Shutterstock.com; pp. 4, 8 (fruit) Valentyn Volkov/Shutterstock.com; pp. 4, 10 (water glass) Elena Elisseeva/Shutterstock.com; p. 5 (pizza) oznuroz/Shutterstock.com; p. 5 (video game) wavebreakmedia ltd/Shutterstock.com; p. 5 (skateboarder) Tomasz Trojanowski/Shutterstock.com; p. 5 (candy) Michael Vitek/Shutterstock.com; p. 7 Ilike/Shutterstock.com; p. 9 Rehan Qureshi/Shutterstock.com; p. 11 Anatoliy Samara/Shutterstock.com; p. 12 MaszaS/Shutterstock.com; p. 13 Africa Studio/Shutterstock.com; p. 14 Rob Marmion/Shutterstock.com.

ISBN: 978-1-4488-8728-6
6-pack ISBN: 978-1-4488-8729-3

Manufactured in the United States of America

CPSIA Compliance Information: Batch #WS12RC: For further information contact Rosen Publishing, New York, New York at 1-800-237-9932.

Word Count: 81

Contents

There are things people need to live.

There are things people want for fun.

I need a safe place to live.

I want a computer in my room.

I need to eat healthy food to live.

I want some ice cream after dinner.

I need to drink water to live.

I want to drink soda with my friends.

I need to wear clothes to stay warm.

I want to wear a pretty necklace.

I need a doctor when I am sick.

Needs and Wants

needs	wants
home	computer
food	ice cream
water	soda
clothes	necklace
doctor	

Words to Know

clothes

computer

doctor

ice cream

necklace

soda

Index